THE FOOTBALL PUZZLE BOOK

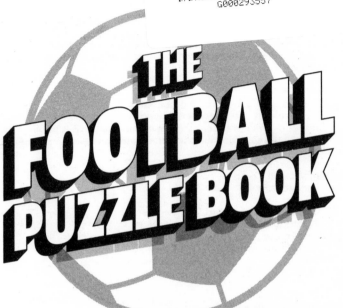

THE FOOTBALL PUZZLE BOOK

Text by Adam Ifans

An Hachette UK Company
www.hachette.co.uk

Summersdale Publishers Ltd
Part of Octopus Publishing Group Limited
Carmelite House
50 Victoria Embankment
LONDON
EC4Y 0DZ
UK

www.summersdale.com

Printed and bound in CPI Group (UK) Ltd, Croydon, CR0 4YY

ISBN: 978-1-80007-921-2

Substantial discounts on bulk quantities of Summersdale books are available to corporations, professional associations and other organizations. For details contact general enquiries: telephone: +44 (0) 1243 771107 or email: enquiries@summersdale.com.

THE FOOTBALL PUZZLE BOOK

BRAIN-TEASING PUZZLES, GAMES AND TRIVIA FOR FOOTBALL FANS

summersdale

INTRODUCTION

Across the globe, football is known as the beautiful game. Whether you're a player or a supporter, there's something about a football pitch that transports you away for 90 minutes to a land where dreams come true – or not, depending on the result!

A kickabout in the local park on a lazy Sunday afternoon can be just as tense as a derby tie in front of nearly 80,000 screaming fans. Football gets under your skin – from playing and supporting to speculating on your team's best players and bemoaning last week's VAR decision – it's all part of the world's greatest sport. It binds friends and family together and gives us something interesting to talk about when we're at work!

This book is a celebration of all things football. From the Premier and Champions Leagues to the World Cup and England Women's Euro 2022 triumph, there's something in here for every football fan, young and old. The pages that follow are packed with puzzles of all sorts, ranging from crosswords and trivia to mazes and riddles.

The Football Puzzle Book is guaranteed to entertain, surprise and delight you in equal measure. It's time to get the game underway...

TRIVIA

The FIFA Golden Boot award is given to the top goalscorer at each World Cup tournament. The award was first called the Golden Boot in 2010 but what was its name before that?

a) The Golden Shoe

b) The Golden Ball

c) The Ballon D'Or

WORD SEARCH

THINGS YOU NEED FOR A FOOTIE GAME

S	E	V	O	L	G	L	D
T	H	E	U	G	O	L	A
R	U	I	B	L	A	A	V
O	R	S	N	O	L	B	T
H	A	T	U	P	S	I	R
S	O	C	K	S	A	R	I
S	T	O	O	B	U	D	H
R	E	F	E	R	E	E	S

Shorts, Goals, Boots, Gloves, Shinpads, Shirt,
Referee, Socks, Ball

CROSSWORD

ENGLAND WOMEN'S 2022 EURO TRIUMPH

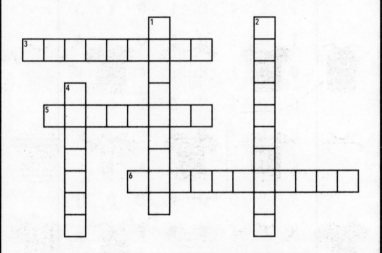

ACROSS

3 Taxi meter (anagram) (5,4)

5 Player of the tournament and top scorer (4,4)

6 Defending champions (11)

DOWN

1 Part of a pride (9)

2 Scored the decisive goal (5,5)

4 The final stage (7)

PAIRS GAME

Match up the 20 football shirts in 20 seconds. The first one has been done for you.

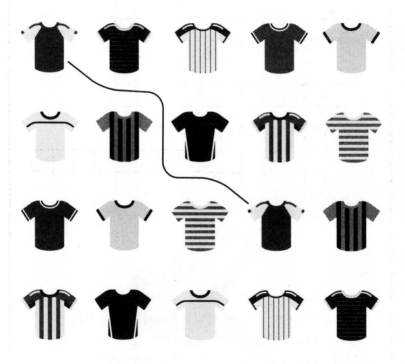

TRIVIA

As a manager, José Mourinho has won two Champion's Leagues and eight league titles with teams in England, Portugal, Spain and Italy. Where did the self-proclaimed Special One start his managerial career?

a) Benfica, Portugal

b) Roma, Italy

c) Porto, Portugal

WORD WHEEL

See how many words of four or more letters you can make from the letters below. All words must include the central letter, and proper nouns don't count! Can you find a word that uses all the letters? You mustn't cross this if you're a manager!

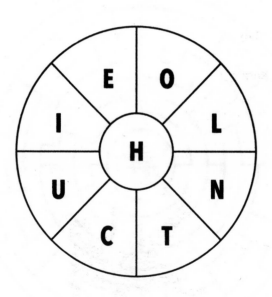

MAZE

Can you help the striker dribble the ball to the goal?

ANAGRAMS
BRILLIANT BRAZILIANS

Rearrange these letters to reveal four Brazilian players who've made it big in the Premier League:

HAND INFERNO

FIBRE OR MONITOR

BALES JUG RISES

SORE END

TRIVIA

The first Women's World Cup had an unusual official name owing to a certain confectionery company's sponsorship. What was it?

a) 1st FIFA World Cup for Women's Football with Galaxy

b) 1st FIFA World Championship for Women's Football for the M&M's Cup

c) FIFA Women's World Cup in association with Kit Kat

WORD LADDER

In this word ladder, change one letter at a time to turn the word FOOT into BALL.

```
FOOT
_ _ _ _
_ _ _ _
_ _ _ _
_ _ _ _
BALL
```

RIDDLE

A trophy-winning manager is the answer to this riddle.

My first is in Sheffield Wednesday and also in Norwich
My second is in kick but not in back pass
My third is in Lineker but not in Ronaldo
My fourth is in goal and also in Agüero
My fifth is in Mead but not in Kelly
My sixth is in penalty but not in strike
My seventh is in Kane and also in Mukandi

Who am I?

DOT-TO-DOT

Join the dots to find the mystery image.

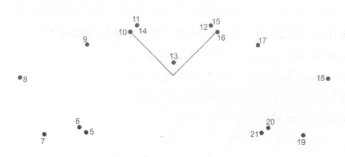

TRIVIA

La Masia is a Spanish youth academy that's famous for producing players such as Andrés Iniesta and Xavi. Which football team runs La Masia?

a) Atlético Madrid

b) Real Madrid

c) Barcelona

SPOT THE DIFFERENCE

Can you find the ten differences between these two pictures?

REBUS

What a goal! She's hit the...

!TEN EHT FO

MISSING VOWELS

Here are the names of some famous male footballers – past and present – with the vowels deleted. Can you work out who they are?

DVDBCKHM

PL

ZC

NYMR

LK MDRC

LN SHRR

NDRS NST

GR LNKR

JMM GRVS

HRR KN

TRIVIA

Which of these famous players did not play for Arsenal Women's team in the 2021–22 season?

a) Vivianne Miedema

b) Beth Mead

c) Lisa Evans

COUNTING CONUNDRUM

⚽ + ⚽ = 28

👟 + 🧤 = 16

👟 + ⚽ = 25

⚽ = ?

👟 = ?

🧤 = ?

CROSSWORD

NAME THAT TEAM

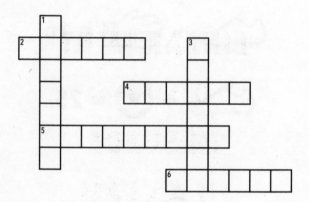

ACROSS

2 An original Briton (6)
4 They hunt in packs (6)
5 A recent fortress (9)
6 A chap who's
  got it together (3,3)

DOWN

1 You're doing
  this right now (7)
3 Where the oranges come
  from (7)

ANAGRAMS
ITALIAN CLUBS

Rearrange these letters to reveal four famous Serie A regulars:

LINEAR MINT

OIL PAN

IN SUEDE

IN A CLAM

TRIVIA

Wembley is England's biggest football stadium, holding 90,000 spectators. Which Premier League team plays at the second biggest?

a) Liverpool

b) Manchester United

c) Arsenal

RIDDLE

The first country to win the World Cup is the answer to this riddle.

My first is in ground and also in turf
My second is in defender but not in goalie
My third is in United but not in City
My fourth is in kicking and also in throwing
My fifth is in cup but not in trophy
My sixth is in Carrow and also in Road
My seventh is in Stanway but not in White

What am I?

WORD WHEEL

See how many words of four or more letters you can make from the letters below. All words must include the central letter, and proper nouns don't count! Can you find a word that uses all the letters? You'll need plenty of these for training!

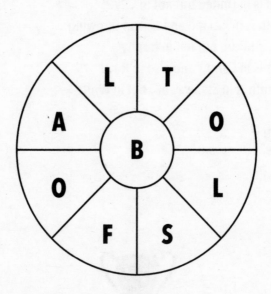

DOT-TO-DOT

Join the dots to find the mystery image.

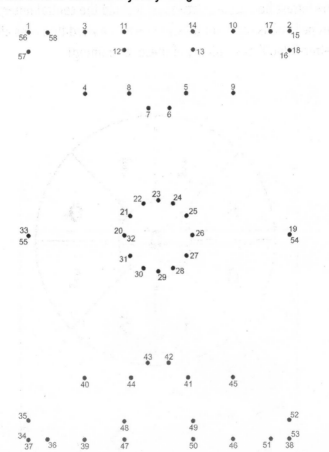

SPOT THE DIFFERENCE

Can you find the ten differences between these two pictures?

MISSING VOWELS

Here are the names of ten famous English football grounds with the vowels removed. Can you work out where they are?

GDSN PRK

STM FR DBR DG

WMBL STDM

LLND RD

NFLD

SLHRST PRK

STDM F LGHT

BRMLL LN

CRRW RD

ST JMS PRK

PAIRS GAME

Match up the 20 footballers in 20 seconds. The first one has been done for you.

WORD SEARCH

ROLES ON THE PITCH

```
F  A  L  S  E  N  I  N  E  L  D  N  B  B
M  R  G  N  R  D  Z  R  T  L  L  B  B  K
R  E  P  E  E  K  L  A  O  G  X  V  C  D
R  X  S  J  T  R  X  T  K  K  X  A  S  X
R  E  K  T  Z  Y  Z  P  W  B  B  E  W  K
Q  K  D  M  R  Q  Q  T  T  G  N  R  E  C
P  L  Q  L  Y  I  L  J  N  T  E  Q  E  A
N  K  N  R  E  D  K  I  R  K  J  P  P  B
R  M  M  G  W  I  W  E  A  N  Y  M  E  E
E  R  G  Q  K  V  F  M  R  X  D  B  R  R
G  Z  W  Z  L  B  Y  D  T  N  R  B  D  T
N  K  J  D  A  A  T  X  I  P  N  V  T  N
I  J  L  C  L  Y  P  D  N  M  M  J  K  E
W  W  K  P  G  Q  B  D  Q  D  N  R  Q  C
```

Goalkeeper, Centre-Back, Wing-Back, Midfielder, Striker,
Playmaker, False Nine, Sweeper, Winger

TRIVIA

Singer-songwriter Ed Sheeran was the men's and women's first team shirt sponsor for which football club in 2022?

a) Norwich

b) Ipswich

c) West Bromwich Albion

WORD LADDER

In this word ladder, change one letter at a time to turn the word KICKS into KEEPS.

KICKS

_ _ _ _ _

_ _ _ _ _

_ _ _ _ _

_ _ _ _ _

KEEPS

MAZE

Can you help the team bus get to the ground?

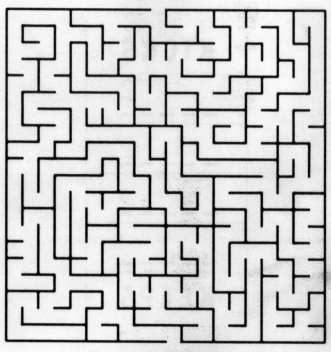

COUNTING CONUNDRUM

$a + b = 8$
$a + c = 11$
$b + c = 9$

(A) 🏆 (5) + (3) 🛡 (B) = 8

(6)

(5) 🏆 + ⬜ (6) = 11

(B 9) 🛡 (3) + ⬜ (6) = 9

$2a + B + c = 19$
$2c + a + b = 20$

🏆 = ? 5

🛡 = ? 3

⬜ = ? 6

TRIVIA

Fran Kirby scored a brace in a 5-0 against Benfica in the Women's Champions League which made her the top all-time goalscorer for her club. Who was she playing for?

a) Arsenal

b) Everton

c) Chelsea

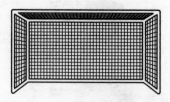

REBUS

The game was won during…

JU TIME RY

CROSSWORD

WORLD CUP 1966

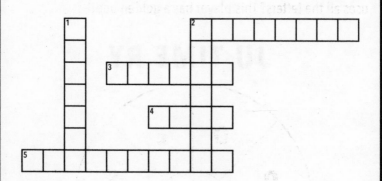

ACROSS

2 They beat the Soviets to claim third place (8)
3 The World Cup was boycotted by this continent (6)
4 All the action happened in this month (4)
5 The hat-trick hero (5,5)

DOWN

1 Top scorer in the finals (7)
2 The dog who found the trophy (7)

WORD WHEEL

See how many words of four or more letters you can make from the letters below. All words must include the central letter, and proper nouns don't count! Can you find a two-word phrase that uses all the letters? This player has a golden boot!

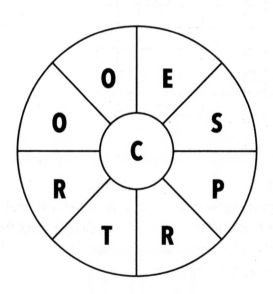

TRIVIA

In the 1970s, Ajax and the Netherlands popularized a style of football that relied on every player being able to play every role on the pitch apart from the goalkeeper. What was this style called?

a) Ultimate Football

b) Absolute Football

c) Total Football

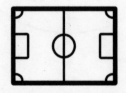

ANAGRAMS
WOMEN'S SUPER LEAGUE
HOTSHOTS

Rearrange these letters to reveal four players with an eye for goal:

BAD THEME

ARCHED ALLY

INVASIVE IS YEA

INSULTS IN BACKSEAT

DOT-TO-DOT

Join the dots to find the mystery image.

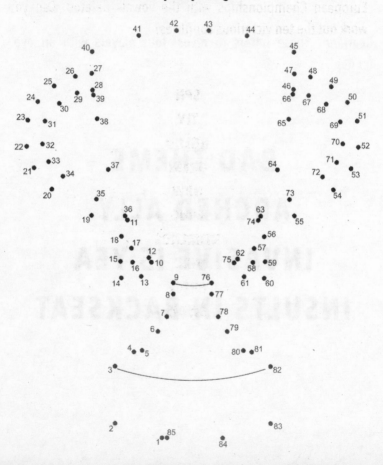

MISSING VOWELS

Here are the names of some winners of the men's and women's European Championships with the vowels deleted. Can you work out the ten victorious countries?

SPN

TLY

NGLND

GRMN

NRW

FRNC

NTHRLNDS

GRC

PRTGL

SWDN

TRIVIA

The Premier League kicked off in autumn 1992 but which club won the last ever Division One title in the 1991/92 season?

a) Blackburn Rovers

b) Leeds United

c) Manchester United

SPOT THE DIFFERENCE

Can you find the ten differences between these two pictures?

WORD LADDER

In this word ladder, change one letter at a time to turn the word BOOTS into FOULS.

BOOTS

_ _ _ _ _

_ _ _ _ _

_ _ _ _ _

_ _ _ _ _

FOULS

PAIRS GAME

Match up the 20 medals in 20 seconds. The first one has been done for you.

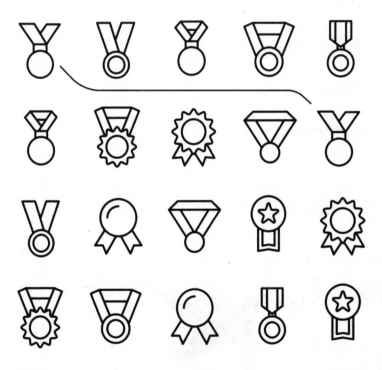

TRIVIA

Which famous manager said: "Some people believe football is a matter of life and death. I'm very disappointed with that attitude. I can assure you it is much, much more important than that."?

a) Brian Clough

b) Jürgen Klopp

c) Bill Shankly

WORD SEARCH

EUROPEAN CLUBS

D	I	R	D	A	M	L	A	E	R
M	O	A	D	S	V	I	L	A	Q
F	A	I	L	O	P	A	N	O	S
A	M	R	A	W	E	O	P	S	U
C	I	V	S	A	L	B	O	R	T
I	L	A	M	E	D	U	R	K	N
F	A	Y	C	B	I	L	T	O	E
N	N	R	H	O	L	L	O	D	V
E	A	R	T	G	B	U	L	G	U
B	L	E	I	P	Z	I	G	E	J

Porto, Barcelona, Marseille, Milan, Real Madrid,
Juventus, Benfica, Leipzig, Napoli

COUNTING CONUNDRUM

x = 9

+ = 20

− = 7

= ?

= ?

= ?

REBUS

Football is a...

$$\frac{GA}{2} \quad \frac{ME}{2}$$

TRIVIA

When Harry Redknapp's West Ham team played a 1994 pre-season friendly in Oxford, the manager substituted one of his players and put on:

a) A fan who'd been complaining about the player

b) An opposing player who was still on the bench

c) Himself, but only to take a last-minute throw-in

MAZE

Can you help the captain lift the trophy?

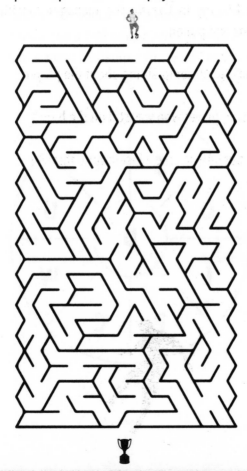

WORD WHEEL

See how many words of four or more letters you can make from the letters below. All words must include the central letter, and proper nouns don't count! Can you find a two-word phrase that uses all the letters? They only happen 25 times a century!

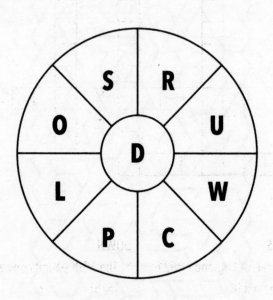

CROSSWORD

PENALTIES

ACROSS

3 In goal for England's 2021 Euro final (8)

5 Another name for the spot (7,4)

6 He wore a paper bag after missing in a shootout (9)

DOWN

1 The 11th penalty onward (6, 5)

2 Bruce Grobbelaar's legs (9)

2 It was invented in this green land (7)

TRIVIA

Which team won the Women's Super League in 2021-22, with striker Sam Kerr netting 20 times during the season?

a) Arsenal

b) Manchester City

c) Chelsea

RIDDLE

Two footballing brothers are the answer to this riddle.

My first is in Charles and also in Buchanon
My second is in Harry but not in Kane
My third is in Neymar but not in Messi
My fourth is in pride and also in tribe
My fifth is in flag but not in corner
My sixth is in Stones and also in Le Tissier
My seventh is in Orman but not in Fleming
My eighth is in nutmeg and also in defender

Who am I?

DOT-TO-DOT

Join the dots to find the mystery image.

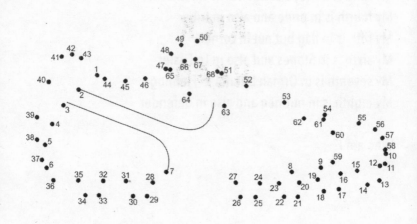

REBUS

Beth Mead scored the winner with an…

KICK

HEAD

SPOT THE DIFFERENCE

Can you find the ten differences between these two pictures?

MISSING VOWELS

Here are the names of some famous female footballers — past and present — with the vowels deleted. Can you work out all ten?

LLN WHT

MCHLL KRS

KLL SMTH

BB WMBCH

BTH MD

MGN RPN

CHL KLL

MRT

LCY BRNZ

NDN NGRR

COUNTING CONUNDRUM

$$\frac{\text{🧤}}{2} = 1$$

$$\text{🧤} + \text{🏆} = 14$$

$$\text{⚽} - \text{🏆} = 1$$

$$\text{🧤} = ?$$

$$\text{🏆} = ?$$

$$\text{⚽} = ?$$

TRIVIA

Which of these is not the name for an acrobatic overhead kick?

a) Bicycle

b) Catapult

c) Scorpion

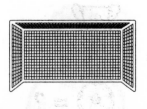

TRIVIA

Bobby Moore captained the World Cup 1966 winning England team and played over 600 games for West Ham. Which London rival does he share a middle name with?

a) Fulham

b) Charlton

c) Chelsea

ANAGRAMS
ENGLAND MANAGERS

Rearrange these letters to reveal four coaches who have sat in the England hotseat:

LEND GOLD HEN

GEEK IN KNAVE

EVIL PIN HELL

DEAL MY RASCAL

WORD SEARCH

ENGLISH CLUBS

G	L	O	O	P	R	E	V	I	L
A	D	I	B	S	R	T	D	A	B
M	T	G	N	I	D	A	E	R	Y
A	U	S	T	C	E	S	O	S	T
H	N	O	L	K	L	O	P	E	I
T	A	I	O	E	T	J	D	N	C
S	M	E	H	T	S	A	E	A	N
E	M	C	S	G	H	A	W	L	A
W	O	N	O	T	R	E	V	E	M
A	L	L	I	V	N	O	T	S	A

Arsenal, Chelsea, Everton, West Ham, Reading, Man Utd,
Man City, Aston Villa, Liverpool

WORD LADDER

In this word ladder, change one letter at a time to turn the word BACK into HEEL.

BACK

_ _ _ _

_ _ _ _

_ _ _ _

_ _ _ _

HEEL

TRIVIA

Which England football manager was cruelly nicknamed Turnip by *The Sun* newspaper?

a) Howard Wilkinson

b) Steve McClaren

c) Graham Taylor

RIDDLE

A cherished prize is the answer to this riddle.

My first is in fan and also in gaffer
My second is in Walsh but not in Bronze
My third is in accurate but not in passing
My fourth is in Russo and also in Fulham
My fifth is in Parris but not in Kirby

What am I?

PAIRS GAME

Match up the 20 lions in 20 seconds. The first one has been done for you.

MAZE

Can you help the supporter find the pie?

TRIVIA

World Cup 2015 winners, United States, were honoured with a ticker-tape parade on their return to their homeland. To which city did they get the key?

a) Washington, D.C.

b) Los Angeles

c) New York

CROSSWORD

THE CHAMPIONS LEAGUE

ACROSS

2 The first British team to lift the cup (6)
4 The most successful club (4,6)
5 Name of the second-tier competition (6)
6 Player with most appearances (7)

DOWN

1 This is trophy material (6)
3 It was called this until 1992 (8,3)

DOT-TO-DOT

Join the dots to find the mystery image.

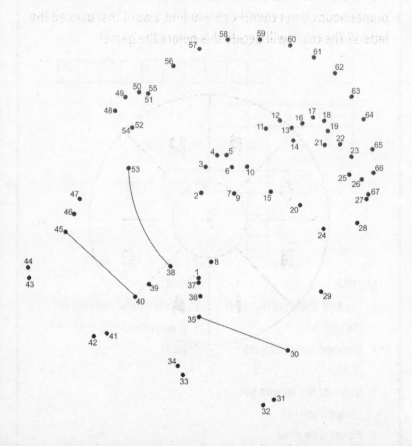

WORD WHEEL

See how many words of four or more letters you can make from the letters below. All words must include the central letter, and proper nouns don't count! Can you find a word that uses all the letters? The coach will decide this before the game!

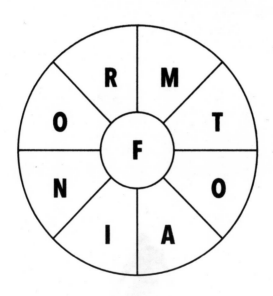

TRIVIA

What is the name for the football skill where the player in possession passes it through the legs of an opposing player?

a) Clove

b) Nutmeg

c) Ginger

REBUS

You get a penalty when there's a…

BOFOULX

COUNTING CONUNDRUM

$$\text{trophy} + \text{shirt} = 5$$

$$\text{shirt} - \text{trophy} = 1$$

$$\text{boot} \times \text{trophy} = 100$$

$$\text{trophy} = ?$$

$$\text{shirt} = ?$$

$$\text{boot} = ?$$

SPOT THE DIFFERENCE

Can you find the ten differences between these two pictures?

TRIVIA

Which superstar footballer said: "A penalty is a cowardly way to score"?

a) Michel Platini

b) Pelé

c) Lionel Messi

MISSING VOWELS

Here are the names of ten winners of the Premier League Golden Boot, with the vowels deleted. Can you work out all top scorers?

TDD SHRNGHM

ND CL

THRR HNR

RD VN NSTLRY

DDR DRGB

JM VRD

MHMD SLH

NCLS NLK

RBN VN PRS

SRG GR

ANAGRAMS
WELSH WONDERS

Rearrange these letters to reveal four Welsh players who've set the football world on fire over the years:

SUN HAIR

BAGEL HEART

AREA MASONRY

HUG ME SHARK

WORD SEARCH

WORLD CUP FINALISTS

```
A  F  R  A  N  C  E  C  A
H  R  U  N  G  E  N  R  Y
U  S  G  I  F  E  G  O  N
N  E  S  I  D  E  L  A  A
G  R  A  E  N  B  A  T  M
A  B  W  T  R  D  N  I  R
R  S  I  E  L  I  D  A  E
Y  N  L  I  Z  A  R  B  G
A  U  R  U  G  U  A  Y  E
```

Brazil, England, Hungary, France, Argentina, Germany,
Uruguay, Sweden, Croatia

TRIVIA

Scudetto is the nickname for which European country's top football championship?

a) Portugal

b) Spain

c) Italy

WORD LADDER

In this word ladder, change one letter at a time to turn the word GRASS into POSTS.

GRASS

_ _ _ _ _

_ _ _ _ _

_ _ _ _ _

_ _ _ _ _

_ _ _ _ _

POSTS

PAIRS GAME

Match up the 20 football badges in 20 seconds. The first one has been done for you.

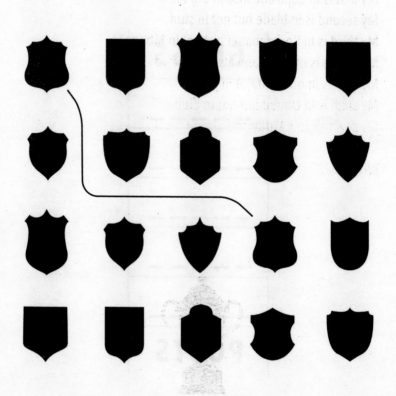

RIDDLE

A gift that comes in a box is the answer to this riddle.

My first is in Copa and also in Del Piero
My second is in blade but not in stud
My third is in Beckenbauer but not in Mbappé
My fourth is in Salah and also in Hazard
My fifth is in goal but not in keeper
My sixth is in United but not in Club
My seventh is in Vardy and also in Yashin

What am I?

TRIVIA

England player, Lucy Bronze, joined Barcelona on a free transfer in the summer of 2022. But which English club did she previously play for?

a) Everton

b) Manchester City

c) Liverpool

MAZE

Can you help the referee find his whistle?

SPOT THE DIFFERENCE

Can you find the ten differences between these two pictures?

MISSING VOWELS

Here are the names of some famous football grounds across the globe, with the vowels deleted. Can you work out where in the world they are?

SN SR

SNTG BRNB

CMP N

STD LMPC

L BMBNR

STD D LZ

MRCN

STD D FRNC

JHN CRFF RN

STD MNMNTL

TRIVIA

"Heavy metal football" is a high intensity style of play with fast counter-attacking moves. Which international manager brought it to the Premier League?

a) Jürgen Klopp

b) Erik ten Hag

c) Mauricio Pochettino

REBUS

She's got a... with the keeper!

1

1

COUNTING CONUNDRUM

$$\text{goal} + \text{goal} = 22$$

$$\text{player} + \text{shorts} = 9$$

$$\text{player} + \text{goal} = 100$$

$$\text{goal} = ?$$

$$\text{player} = ?$$

$$\text{shorts} = ?$$

CROSSWORD

MATCH DAY ESSENTIALS

ACROSS

4 You'll get it in the neck if you don't have one of these (5)

5 Match of the Day, for example (9)

6 Wear the same with pride (7,5)

DOWN

1 A split-second steak and kidney (4,4,3)

2 The whole schedule of games to be played (7,4)

3 Show it at the gate (6)

TRIVIA

England kicked off the Women's Euro 2022 tournament with a 1–0 win over Austria. Where was it played?

a) Old Trafford

b) Wembley

c) Bramall Lane

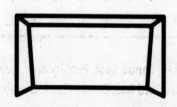

WORD SEARCH

ON THE PITCH

```
C O L T O P S E R T N E C H
T O U L D F A R A D V B N A
M A R G H D H N G B O X T L
S D E N C V E S V B J O K F
X W N R E N H E N O U I O W
O K I P A R C V B C W J K A
B I L L U Y F I H S G L C Y
D V L A J L T L W E R N S L
R E A G H L I L A S T I H I
A L O O G N O A A G H J K N
Y A G E E B A E R N O C R E
X E R A B S S O R C E S D J
I S D P A T Y U X O B P H B
S C E N T R E C I R C L E F
```

Corner Flag, Centre Spot, Penalty Area, Goal Line,
Halfway Line, Six Yard Box, Centre Circle, Crossbar, Touchline

WORD WHEEL

See how many words of four or more letters you can make from the letters below. All words must include the central letter, and proper nouns don't count! Can you find a two-word phrase that uses all the letters? The manager is often called this by the players!

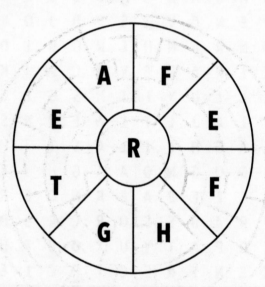

MAZE

Can you help the mascot get to the centre spot?

TRIVIA

Arsenal fans celebrate a special feast day, held on the date that it becomes mathematically impossible for Tottenham Hotspur to finish above them in the league. The celebration is held on a different date every year – and sometimes doesn't happen at all – but what is its name?

a) St Hotspur's Feast

b) St Spurned's Festival

c) St Totteringham's Day

ANAGRAMS
SPANISH CLUBS

Rearrange these letters to reveal four of LaLiga's most famous clubs:

COBRA LANE
RED ADMIRAL
BIBLICAL HOT TEA
NICE LAVA

DOT-TO-DOT

Join the dots to find the mystery image.

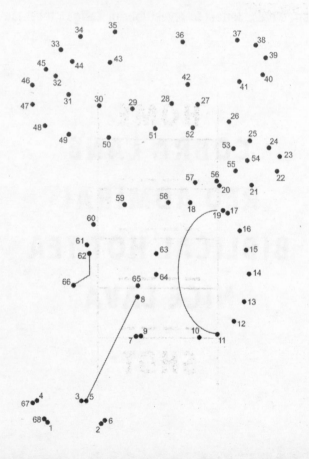

WORD LADDER

In this word ladder, change one letter at a time to turn the word HOME into SHOT.

HOME

_ _ _ _

_ _ _ _

_ _ _ _

_ _ _ _

SHOT

PAIRS GAME

Match up the 20 football trophies in 20 seconds. The first one has been done for you.

RIDDLE

A football club that's full of energy is the answer to this riddle.

My first is in Stoke and also in Southampton
My second is in touchline but not in football
My third is in De Bruyne but not in Coutinho
My fourth is in badge and also in goal
My fifth is in Lampard but not in Rodríguez
My sixth is in Saturday and also in sport

What am I?

MISSING VOWELS

Here are the names of some winners of the World Cup Golden Boot award, with the vowels deleted. Can you work out all these hotshot men and women?

THMS MLLR
BRGT PRNZ
RNLD
CL SSC
PL RSS
SSS
MRSLV KLS
HMR SW
SLVTR SCHLLC
SN WN

REBUS

They're using a 4-4-2...

MATION   **MATION**

MATION   **MATION**

TRIVIA

England legend, David Beckham, is co-owner of Major League Soccer side Inter Miami in the United States. Which other club does he co-own, a little closer to his roots?

a) Rochdale

b) Leigh United

c) Salford City

COUNTING CONUNDRUM

⚽ x 🧤 = 6

⚽ + 🏆 = 14

🧤 + 🏆 = 13

⚽ = ?

🧤 = ?

🏆 = ?

SPOT THE DIFFERENCE

Can you find the ten differences between these two pictures?

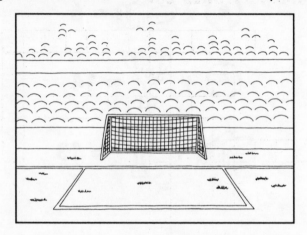

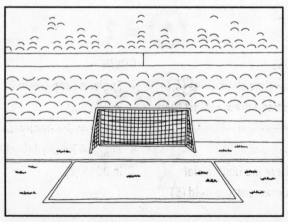

CROSSWORD

WOMEN'S WORLD CUP

ACROSS
1 Four-time champions (6,6)
5 Scotland drew against them for their only World Cup finals point (9)
6 Where the first official tournament was held (5)

DOWN
2 England's top scorer in 2019 (5,5)
3 Shape of the trophy (6)
4 England finished third here in 2015 (6)

TRIVIA

England made it to the semi-finals in the 2015 Women's World Cup. Which team did they lose to after an own goal in injury time?

a) United States

b) Japan

c) Germany

WORD WHEEL

See how many words of four or more letters you can make from the letters below. All words must include the central letter, and proper nouns don't count! Can you find a three-word phrase that uses all the letters? It's how Maradona scored *that* goal in 1986!

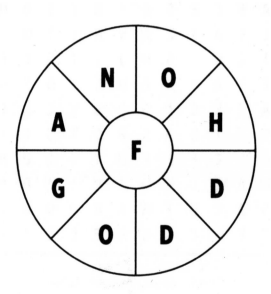

WORD SEARCH

CLUB NICKNAMES

```
C H A M M E R S F G O S
K L I K S J O I W A Z P
A E C E S A I N T S O H
L S A T E W V N L T M I
I G N I G H J L T N C E
E T A Y H F U E J O P N
A E R G I G R B V C K C
R E I K A S B O T S L I
A S E E F F O T E L U B
M A S L K U T R I W D P
S A L U T W A R Y O M A
G E S E L G A E E S L E
```

Canaries, Saints, Hammers, Toffees
Seagulls, Owls, Rams, Potters, Eagles

ANAGRAMS
WORLD BEATERS

Rearrange these letters to reveal four of FIFA's best players of the year:

BLUR COY ZEN

OWLS TO WINDBREAKER

LONE MISSILE

AXES ILL PLATEAU

RIDDLE

A footballing genius is the answer to this riddle.

My first is in trophy and also in penalty
My second is in Müller but not in Platini
My third is in ball but not in boot
My fourth is in Liverpool and also in Everton

Who am I?

DOT-TO-DOT

Join the dots to find the mystery image.

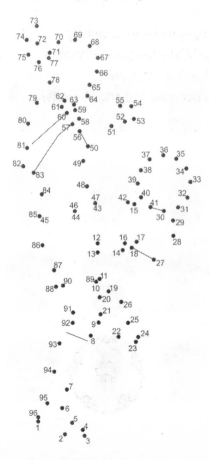

PAIRS GAME

Match up the 20 football shirts in 20 seconds. The first one has been done for you.

TRIVIA

Which forthright pundit said of Manchester United's young team in 1995, "You can't win anything with kids"?

a) Graeme Souness

b) Gary Lineker

c) Alan Hansen

WORD LADDER

In this word ladder, change one letter at a time to turn the word
SAVE into DIVE.

SAVE

_ _ _ _

_ _ _ _

DIVE

MAZE

Can you help the goalkeeper find his gloves?

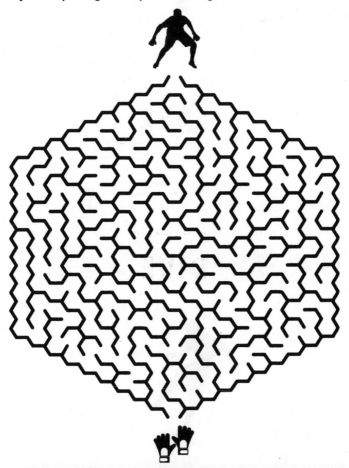

REBUS

PEN S ALTY

H

O

O

T

TRIVIA

Tiki-taka is a style of football that uses quick passing to blow away defences, as practised by the Spanish national side that won Euro 2008, World Cup 2010 and Euro 2012. Which Spanish football manager is it most associated with?

a) Pep Guardiola

b) Robert Moreno

c) Luis Enrique

WORD WHEEL

See how many words of four or more letters you can make from the letters below. All words must include the central letter, and proper nouns don't count! Can you find a two-word phrase that uses all the letters? You'll usually find it just before a penalty shootout!

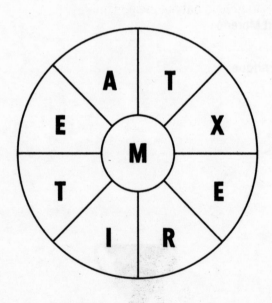

RIDDLE

The first scorer in a final is the answer to this riddle.

My first is in galactico and also in hat trick
My second is in Norwich but not in Ipswich
My third is in boot but not in shirt
My fourth is in Williamson and also in Greenwood
My fifth is in Anfield but not in Spotland

Who am I?

COUNTING CONUNDRUM

$$\text{shoe} \times \text{shoe} = 100$$

$$\text{shoe} \times \text{field} = 1{,}000$$

$$\text{field} \times \text{shirt} = 100{,}000$$

$$\text{shoe} = ?$$

$$\text{field} = ?$$

$$\text{shirt} = ?$$

TRIVIA

Alex Scott made 140 appearances for England and scored the winning goal for Arsenal in the 2007 UEFA Women's Cup Final. After retiring, she finished fifth on which reality television show?

a) *I'm a Celebrity… Get Me Out of Here!*

b) *Strictly Come Dancing*

c) *Dancing on Ice*

SPOT THE DIFFERENCE

Can you find the ten differences between these two pictures?

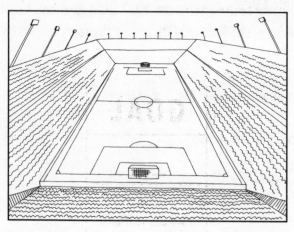

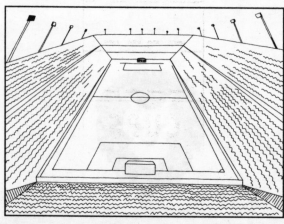

WORD LADDER

In this word ladder, change one letter at a time to turn the word GOAL into CUPS.

GOAL

_ _ _ _

_ _ _ _

_ _ _ _

_ _ _ _

CUPS

ANSWERS

p.6, Trivia
a) The Golden Shoe

p.7, Word Search:

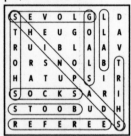

p.8, Crossword
Down: 1 lionesses, 2 Chloe Kelly, 4 Wembley
Across: 3 Extra time, 5 Beth Mead, 6 Netherlands

p.9, Pairs Game

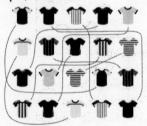

p.10, Trivia
a) Benfica, Portugal

p.11, Word Wheel
Word that uses all letters = touchline

p.12, Maze

p.13, Anagrams
Fernandinho, Roberto Firmino, Gabriel Jesus, Ederson

p.14, Trivia
b) 1st FIFA World Championship for Women's Football for the M&M's Cup

p.15, Word Ladder
One possible solution: foot, fool, tool, toll, tall, ball

p.16, Riddle
Wiegman

p.17, Dot-to-Dot

p.18, Trivia
c) Barcelona

p.19, Spot the Difference

p.20, Rebus
Back of the net!

p.21, Missing Vowels
David Beckham, Pele, Zico, Neymar, Luka Modric, Alan Shearer, Andrés Iniesta, Gary Lineker, Jimmy Greaves, Harry Kane

p.22, Trivia
c) Lisa Evans

p.23, Counting Conundrum
football = 14, boot = 11, glove = 5

p.24, Crossword
Down: 1 Reading, 3 Sevilla
Across: 2 Celtic, 4 Wolves, 5 Newcastle, 6 Man Utd

p.25, Anagrams
Inter Milan, Napoli, Udinese, AC Milan

p.26, Trivia
b) Manchester United

p.27, Riddle
Uruguay

p.28, Word Wheel
Word that uses all letters = footballs

p.29, Dot-to-Dot

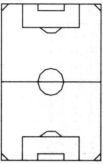

p.30, Spot the Difference

p.31, Missing Vowels
Goodison Park, Stamford Bridge, Wembley Stadium, Elland Road, Anfield, Selhurst Park, Stadium of Light, Bramall Lane, Carrow Road, St James' Park

p.32, Pairs Game

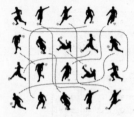

p.33, Word Search

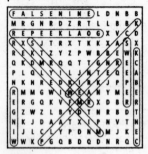

p.34, Trivia
b) Ipswich

p.35, Word Ladder
One possible solution: kicks, picks, pecks, peeks, peeps, keeps

p.36, Maze

p.37, Counting Conundrum
trophy = 5, badge = 3, goal = 6

p.38, Trivia
c) Chelsea

p.39, Rebus
Injury time

p.40, Crossword
Down: 1 Eusébio, 2 Pickles
Across: 2 Portugal, 3 Africa, 4 July, 5 Geoff Hirst

p.41, Word Wheel
Words that use all letters = top scorer

p.42, Trivia
c) Total Football

p.43, Anagrams
Beth Mead, Rachel Daly, Viviane Asseyi, Stina Blackstenius

p.44, Dot-to-Dot

p.45, Missing Vowels

Spain, Italy, England, Germany, Norway, France, Netherlands, Greece, Portugal, Sweden

p.46, Trivia
b) Leeds United

p.47, Spot the Difference

p.48, Word Ladder
One possible solution: boots, books, cooks, cools, fools, fouls

p.49, Pairs Game

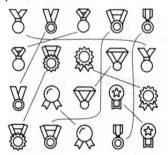

p.50, Trivia
c) Bill Shankly

p.51, Word Search

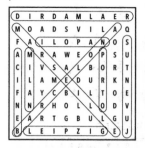

p.52, Counting Conundrum
footballer = 3, shirt = 10, pitch = 17

p.53, Rebus
Game of two halves

p.54, Trivia
a) A fan who'd been complaining about the player

p.55, Maze

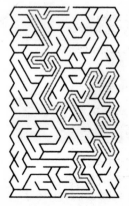

p.56, Word Wheel
Words that use all letters
= world cups

p.57, Crossword
Down: 1 sudden death, 2 spaghetti,
4 Ireland
Across: 3 Pickford, 5 penalty mark,
6 Southgate

p.58, Trivia
c) Chelsea

p.59, Riddle
Charlton

p.60, Dot-to-Dot

p.61, Rebus
Overhead kick

p.62, Spot the Difference

p.63, Missing Vowels
Ellen White, Michelle Akers, Kelly
Smith, Abby Wambach, Beth Mead,

Megan Rapinoe, Chloe Kelly, Marta,
Lucy Bronze, Nadine Angerer

p.64, Counting Conundrum
glove = 2, trophy = 12, football = 13

p.65, Trivia
b) Catapult

p.66, Trivia
c) Chelsea

p.67, Anagrams
Glenn Hoddle, Kevin Keegan, Phil
Neville, Sam Allardyce

p.68, Word Search

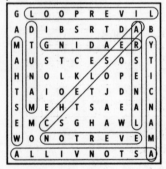

p.69, Word Ladder
One possible solution: back, tack,
talk, tall, tell, hell, heel

p.70, Trivia
c) Graham Taylor

p.71, Riddle
FA Cup

p.72, Pairs Game

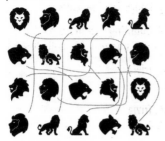

p.73, Maze

p.74, Trivia
c) New York

p.75, Crossword
Down: 1 silver, 3 European Cup
Across: 2 Celtic, 4 Real Madrid, 5 Europa, 6 Ronaldo

p.76, Dot-to-Dot

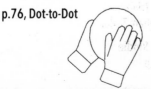

p.77, Word Wheel
Word that uses all letters = formation

p.78, Trivia
b) Nutmeg

p.79, Rebus
Foul in the box

p.80, Counting Conundrum
badge = 2, shirt = 3, boot = 50

p.81, Spot the Difference

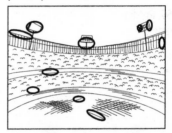

p.82, Trivia
b) Pelé

p.83, Missing Vowels
Teddy Sheringham, Andy Cole, Thierry Henry, Ruud van Nistelrooy, Didier Drogba, Jamie Vardy, Mohamed Salah, Nicolas Anelka, Robin van Persie, Sergio Agüero

p.84, Anagrams
Ian Rush, Gareth Bale, Aaron Ramsey, Mark Hughes

p.85, Word Search

p.86, Trivia
c) Italy

p.87, Word Ladder
One possible solution: grass, brass, brats, boats, coats, costs, posts

p.88, Pairs Game

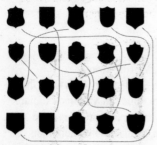

p.89, Riddle
Penalty

p.90, Trivia
b) Manchester City

p.91, Maze

p.92, Spot the Difference

p.93, Missing Vowels
San Siro, Santiago Bernabéu, Camp Nou, Stadio Olimpico, La Bombonera, Estádio da Luz, Maracanã, Stade De France, Johan Cruyff Arena, Estadio Monumental

p.94, Trivia
a) Jürgen Klopp

p.95, Rebus
One-on-one

p.96, Counting Conundrum
goal = 11, footballer = 3, scarf = 6

p.97, Crossword
Down: 1 half time pie, 2 fixture list, 3 ticket
Across: 4 scarf, 5 programme, 6 replica shirt

p.98, Trivia
a) Old Trafford

p.99, Word Search

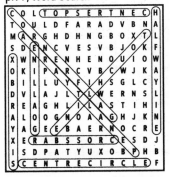

p.100, Word Wheel
Words that use all letters = the gaffer

p.101, Maze

p.102, Trivia
c) St Totteringham's Day

p.103, Anagrams
Barcelona, Real Madrid, Athletic Bilbao, Valencia

p.104, Dot-to-Dot

p.105, Word Ladder
One possible solution: home, hose, host, hoot, soot, shot

p.106, Pairs Game

p.107, Riddle
The Gas

p.108, Missing Vowels
Thomas Müller, Birgit Prinz,
Ronaldo, Célia Šašić, Paolo Rossi,
Sissi, Miroslav Klose, Homare Sawa,
Salvatore Schillaci, Sun Wen

p.109, Rebus
Formation

p.110, Trivia
c) Salford City

p.111, Counting Conundrum
football = 3, glove = 2, trophy = 11

p.112, Spot the Difference

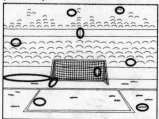

p.113 Crossword
Down: 2 Ellen White, 3 spiral, 4
Canada
Across: 1 United States, 5 Argentina,
6 China

p.114, Trivia
b) Japan

p.115, Word Wheel
Words that use all letters
= hand of god

p.116, Word Search

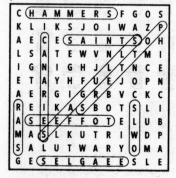

p.117, Anagrams
Lucy Bronze, Robert Lewandowski,
Lionel Messi, Alexia Putellas

p.118, Riddle
Pelé

p.119, Dot-to-Dot

p.120, Pairs Game

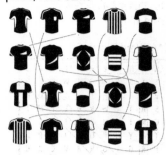

p.121, Trivia
c) Alan Hansen

p.122, Word Ladder
One possible solution: save, gave, give, dive

p.123, Maze

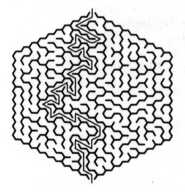

p.124, Rebus
Penalty shootout

p.125, Trivia
a) Pep Guardiola

p.126, Word Wheel
Words that use all letters
= extra time

p.127, Riddle
Toone

p.128, Counting Conundrum
boot = 10, pitch = 100, shirt = 1,000

p.129, Trivia
b) Strictly Come Dancing

p.130, Spot the Difference

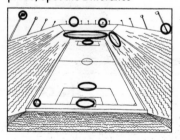

p.131, Word Ladder
One possible solution: coal, cool, coos, cops, cups

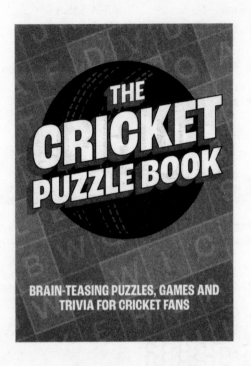

The Cricket Puzzle Book

Paperback

978-1-80007-923-6

Discover word searches, riddles, crosswords, spot-the-differences and much more in this fun-filled activity book for cricket lovers. Whether you're trying to match the pairs of batting gloves or discovering the longest and shortest test matches ever, this book is guaranteed to be a favourite for all who enjoy the game.